THIS WALKER BOOK BELONGS TO:

_____

_____

_____

Chameleons are lizards,
and lizards are reptiles,
like snakes, crocodiles and tortoises.
There are about 4,000 kinds
of lizard altogether, including
around 120 different chameleons.
Just over half of all the kinds
of chameleon come from Madagascar,
a big island off the east coast of Africa.
Most of the others live in
mainland Africa.

For my family M.J.
For Sam and Harry S.S.

First published 1997
by Walker Books Ltd
87 Vauxhall Walk
London SE11 5HJ

2   4   6   8   10   9   7   5   3

Text © 1997 Martin Jenkins
Illustrations © 1997 Sue Shields

This book has been typeset in Calligraphic and Soupbone.

Printed in Hong Kong

British Library Cataloguing in Publication Data:
a catalogue record for this book is
available from the British Library

ISBN 0-7445-6276-7

CHAMELEONS ARE COOL

Martin Jenkins

illustrated by
Sue Shields

WALKER BOOKS

AND SUBSIDIARIES

LONDON • BOSTON • SYDNEY

Geckos' toes are as sticky as Velcro.

Some lizards eat bananas – chameleons don't. Some lizards walk upside down on the ceiling – chameleons can't. There's even a lizard that glides from tree to tree – a chameleon certainly wouldn't do that!

The flying lizard glides on wing-like flaps of skin.

Iguanas don't just eat bananas. They love all sorts of fruit.

But of all the different kinds of lizard,
I still think chameleons are the best.

Chameleons **are** cool.

It's not that they're all that big.
The biggest is only about
the size of a rather small cat.
It's called Oustalet's chameleon
and it lives in Madagascar.

Whatever their size, chameleons usually
get sick and die if kept as pets.
They're much better off left in the wild.

8

They can be really really small, though. The smallest one could balance happily on your little finger. It's called the Dwarf Brookesia, and it lives in Madagascar, too.

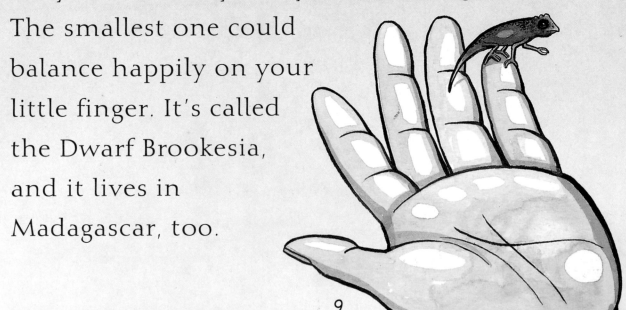

And I suppose you wouldn't exactly call many of them beautiful. Their skin is wrinkly and bumpy, and they've got big bulgy eyes, while lots of them have the most ridiculous...

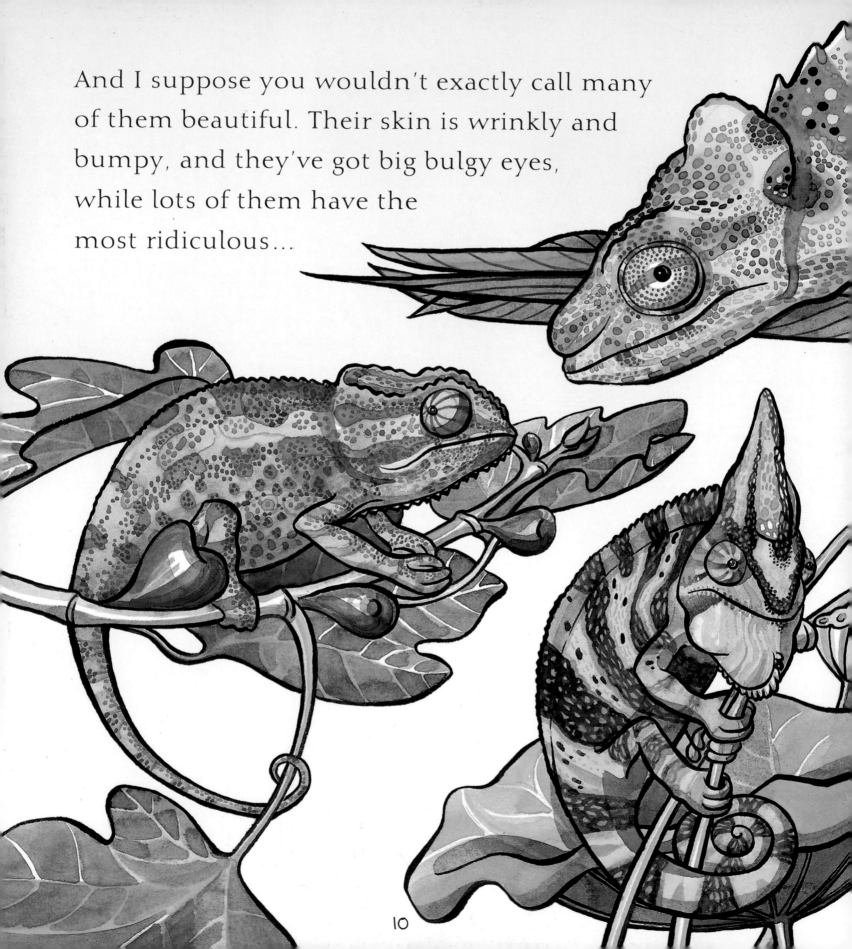

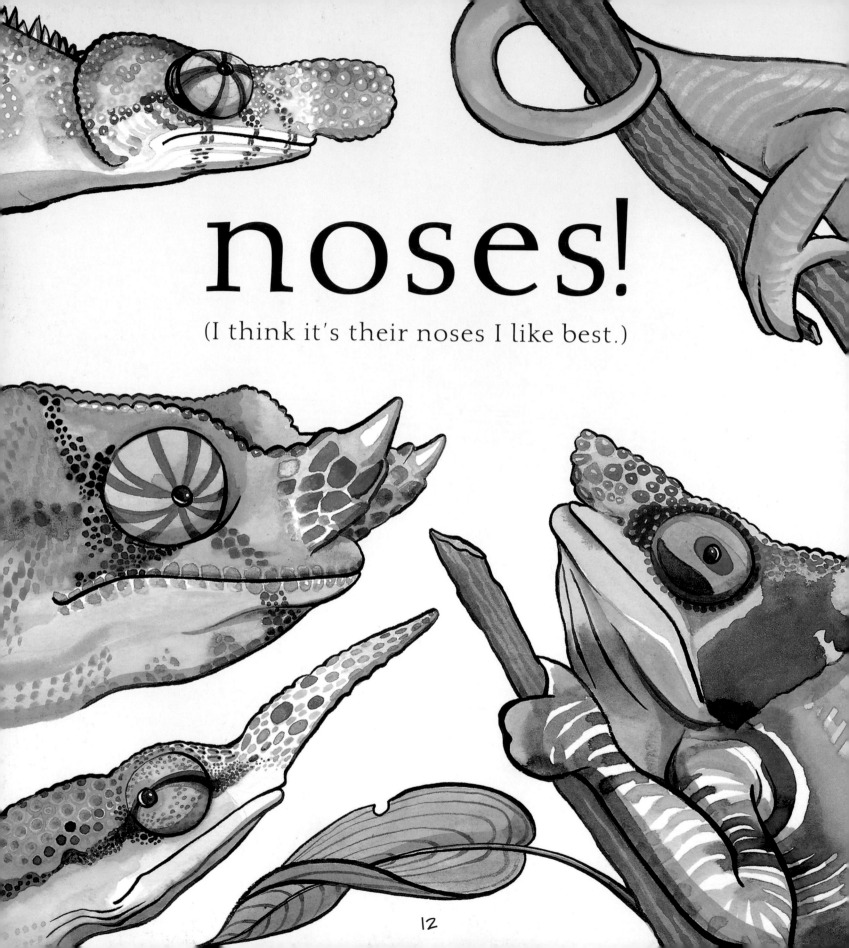

noses!

(I think it's their noses I like best.)

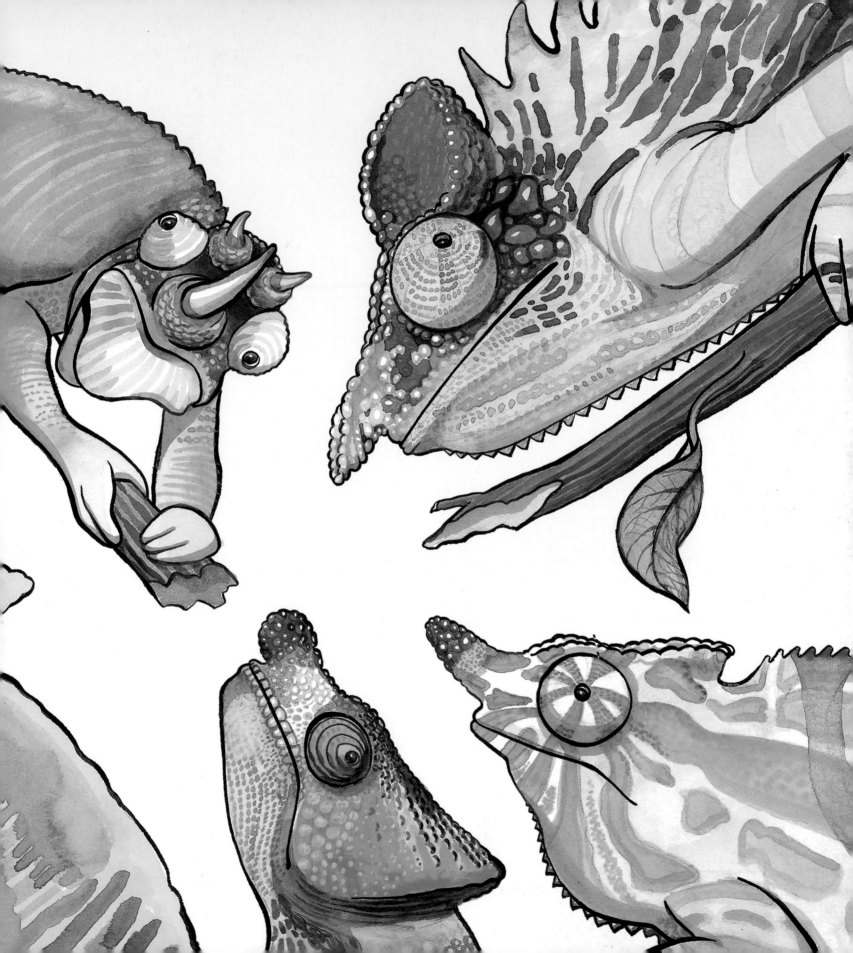

Their mouths are pretty odd, too.
They turn down at the corners,
which is why chameleons
always look grumpy.

Actually they don't just look grumpy.
They **are** grumpy.
So if two chameleons bump into each other,
things can get pretty lively. There's lots
of puffing and hissing – and sometimes,
there's a real fight.

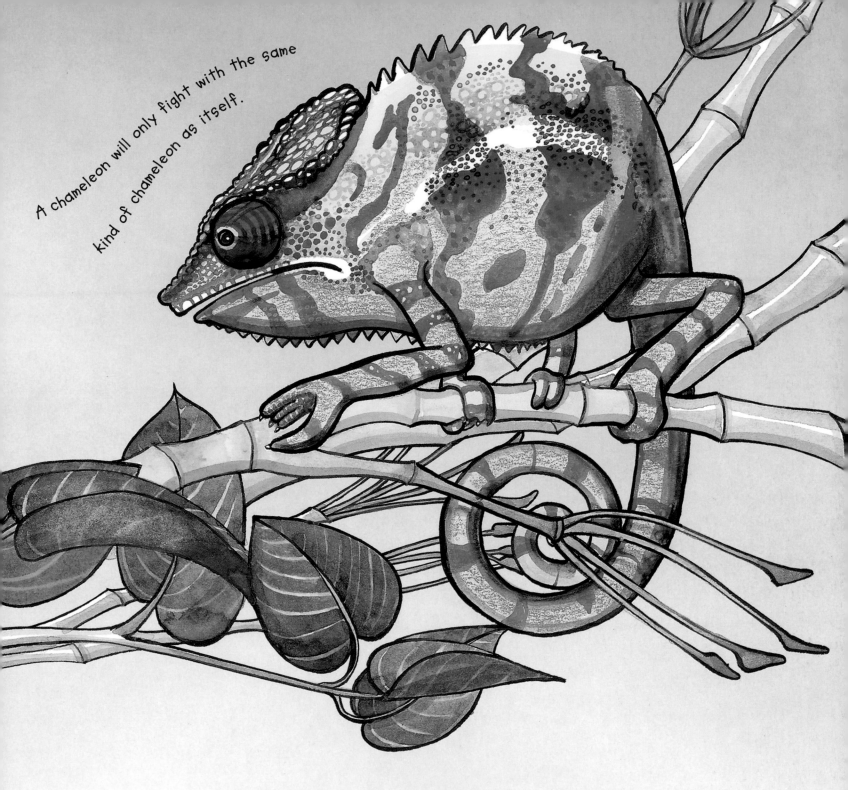

A chameleon will only fight with the same kind of chameleon as itself.

And that's when chameleons do what they're most famous for – they change colour.

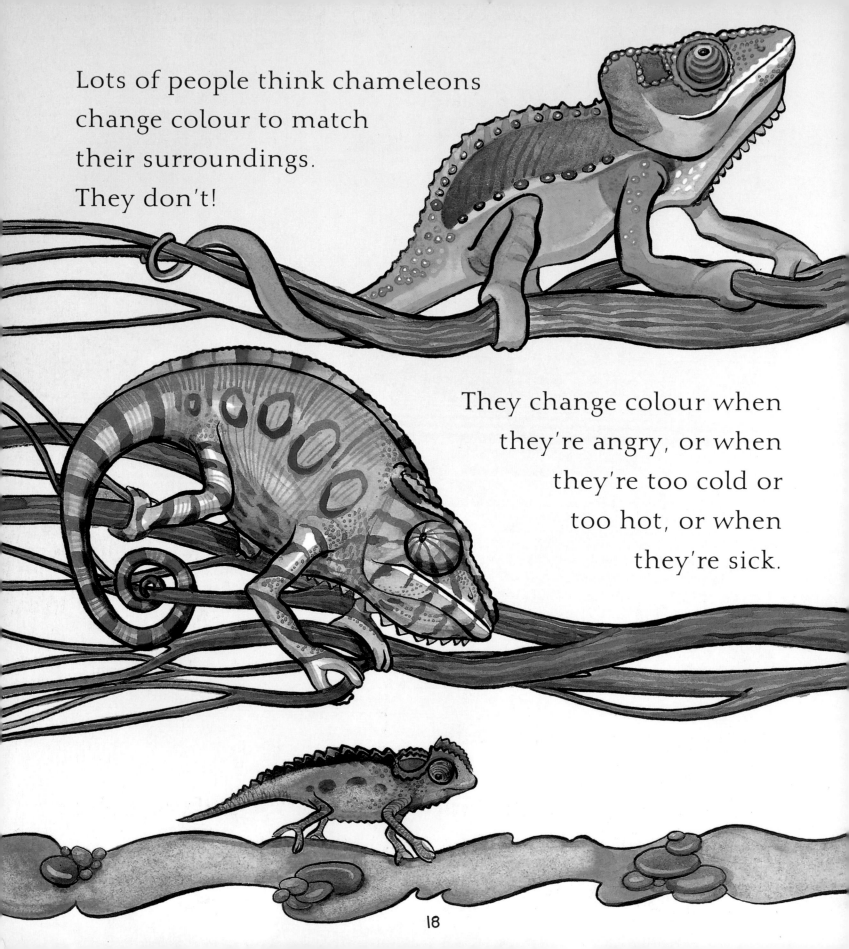

Lots of people think chameleons
change colour to match
their surroundings.
They don't!

They change colour when
they're angry, or when
they're too cold or
too hot, or when
they're sick.

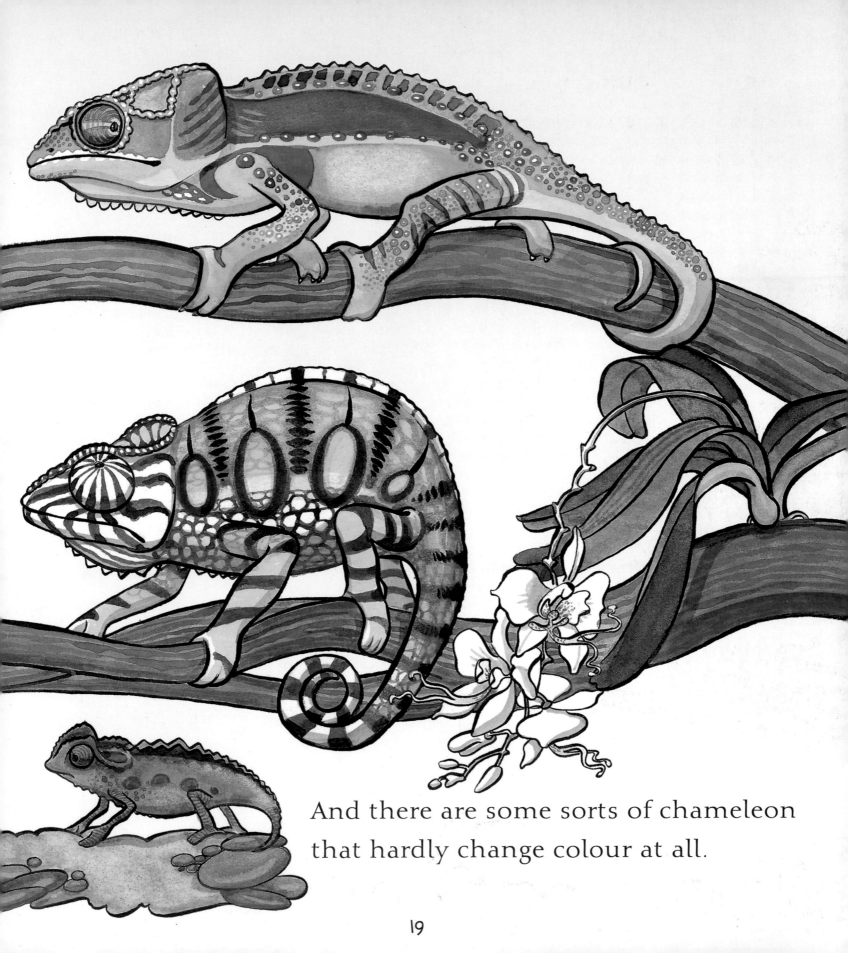

And there are some sorts of chameleon
that hardly change colour at all.

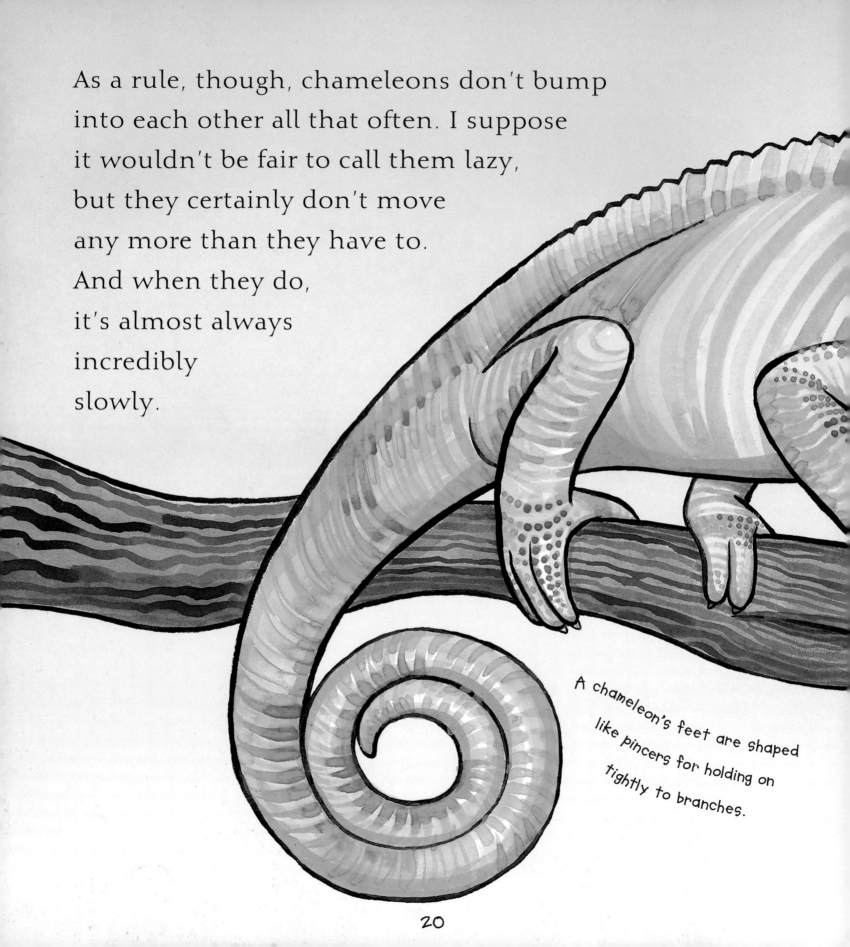

As a rule, though, chameleons don't bump
into each other all that often. I suppose
it wouldn't be fair to call them lazy,
but they certainly don't move
any more than they have to.
And when they do,
it's almost always
incredibly
slowly.

A chameleon's feet are shaped
like pincers for holding on
tightly to branches.

Sometimes they stop completely,
in mid-step, as if they've
quite forgotten what they're
supposed to be doing.

But if you look closely
you'll see that they're actually
carefully peering about.

Now, peering about is something chameleons
are rather good at. That's because
their eyes can move separately
from each other, unlike
our eyes which always
move together.

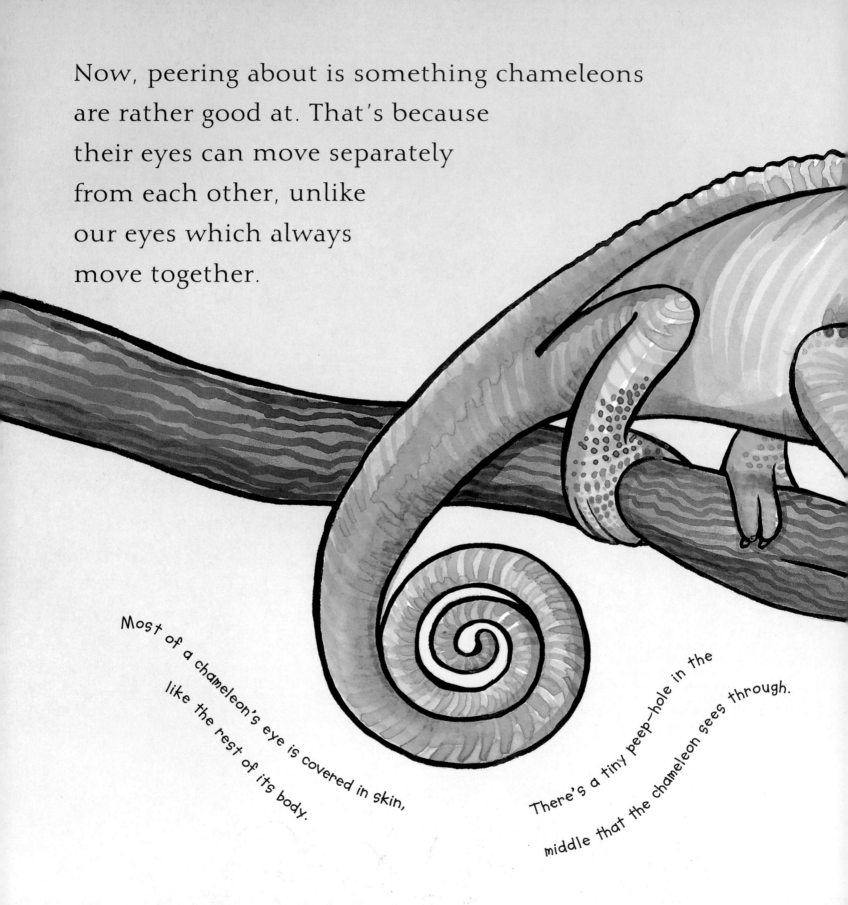

Most of a chameleon's eye is covered in skin,
like the rest of its body.

There's a tiny peep-hole in the
middle that the chameleon sees through.

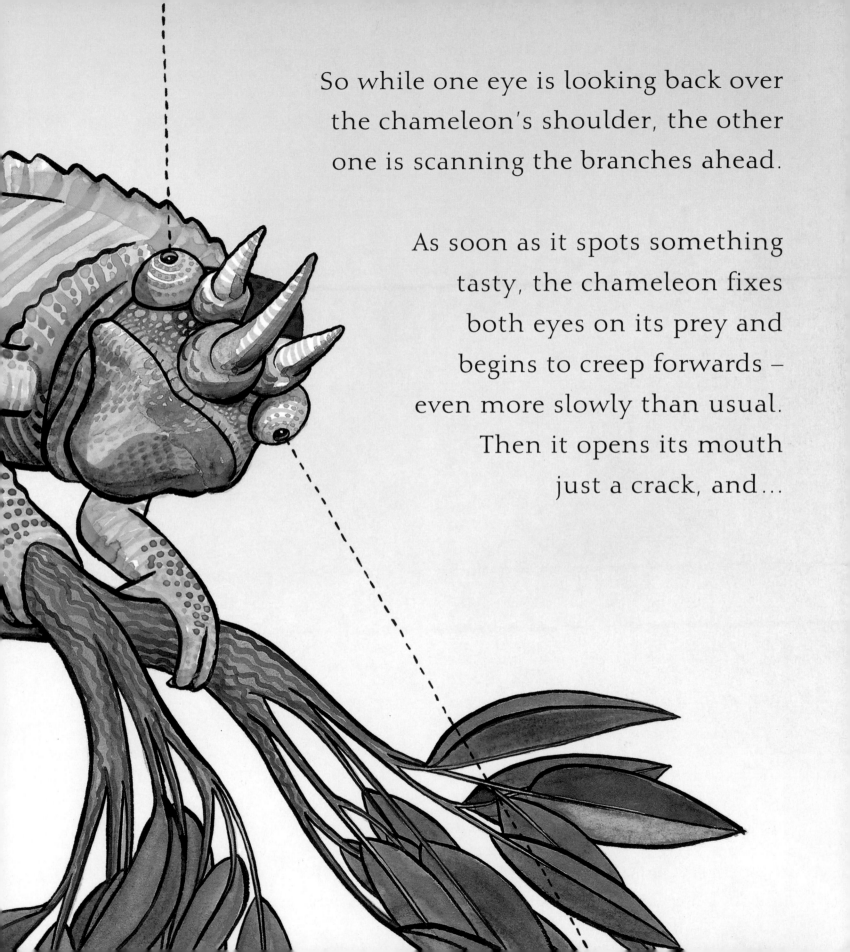

So while one eye is looking back over the chameleon's shoulder, the other one is scanning the branches ahead.

As soon as it spots something tasty, the chameleon fixes both eyes on its prey and begins to creep forwards – even more slowly than usual. Then it opens its mouth just a crack, and...

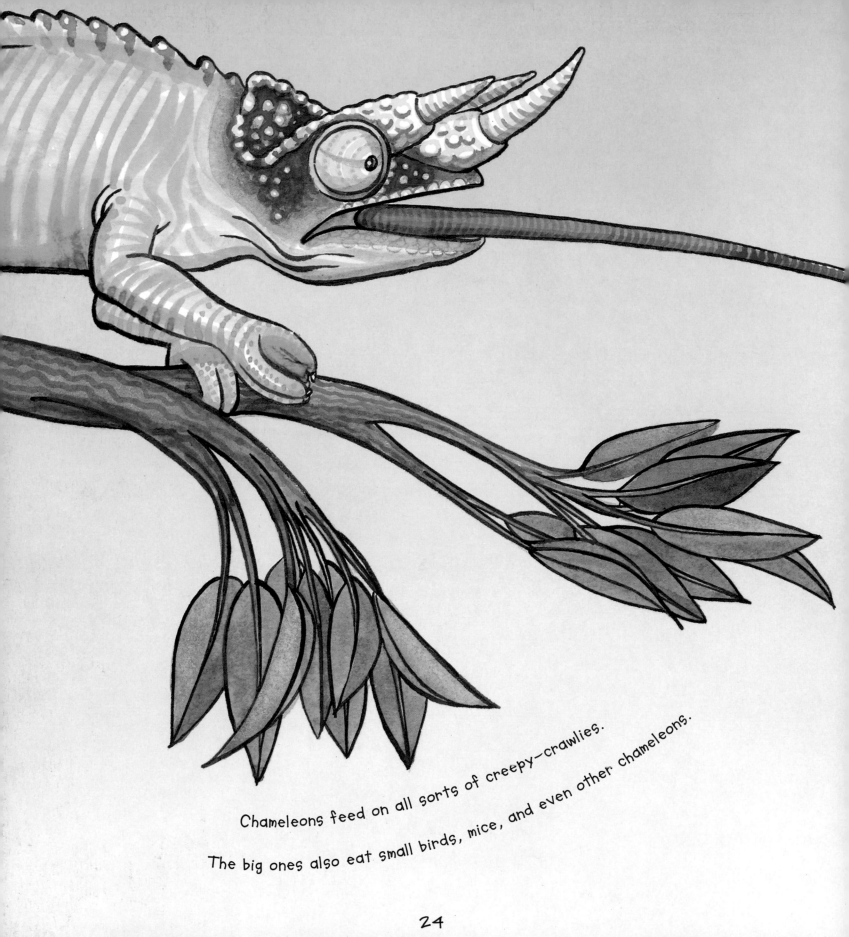

Chameleons feed on all sorts of creepy-crawlies.

The big ones also eat small birds, mice, and even other chameleons.

Out shoots this amazingly long tongue,
with a sticky bit at the end, like a piece
of well-chewed chewing gum.

thwap!

Then the tongue flies back,
and there's a lot
of chomping
and chewing,
and perhaps
a few bits
of insect leg
fluttering to the ground.

Most lizards gulp their food down without chewing it, but chameleons grind everything up thoroughly!

And after that the chameleon just sits there for an hour or two, doing nothing very much at all, looking quite exhausted (and still grumpy) after all that hard work.

And there you have it.
How could you possibly
resist a pocket-sized,
bad-tempered, colour-changing,
swivel-eyed, snail-paced,
long-tongued sharp-shooter?

If chameleons aren't cool,
then I don't know what is!

Index

Look up the pages to find out about
all these chameleon things.
Don't forget to look at both kinds
of word — this kind and this kind.

About the Author

Martin Jenkins is a conservation biologist, who works for
agencies such as the WorldWide Fund for Nature.
"When I first saw chameleons in the wild in Madagascar,"
he recalls, "I fell in love with them at first sight.
I picked one up, ever so gently, and it promptly bit me
on the thumb. I still think they're wonderful, but tend
to leave them alone whenever I bump into them!"
Martin is also the author of *The Emperor's Egg*,
winner of the TES Junior Information Book Award,
Fly Traps! Plants that bite back and *Wings, Stings and Wriggly Things*,
a BRIGHT SPARKS book about minibeasts.

About the Illustrator

Award-winning illustrator Sue Shields has worked
on everything from posters to murals, shop interiors,
magazines, newspapers, greetings cards and children's books.
For *Chameleons are Cool*, she had to adapt her use
of watercolour, "to try to describe not only
their astonishing colours, but a hint of the colours they
can change to". And although she won't give
any names, she says that the chameleons' faces kept
reminding her of people she knows!

NOTES FOR TEACHERS

The READ AND WONDER series is an innovative and versatile resource for reading, thinking and discovery. Each book invites children to become excited about a topic, see how varied information books can be, and want to find out more.

Reading aloud The story form makes these books ideal for reading aloud – in their own right or as part of a cross-curricular topic, to a child or to a whole class. After you've introduced children to the books in this way, they can revisit and enjoy them again and again.

Shared reading Big Book editions are available for several titles, so children can read along, discuss the topic, and comment on the different ways information is presented – to wonder together.

Group and guided reading Children need to experience a range of reading materials. Information books like these help develop the skills of reading to learn, as part of learning to read. With the support of a reading group, children can become confident, flexible readers.

Paired reading It's fun to take turns to read the information in the main text or captions. With a partner, children can explore the pages to satisfy their curiosity and build their understanding.

Individual reading These books can be read for interest and pleasure by children at home and in school.

Research Once children have been introduced to these books through reading aloud, they can use them for independent or group research, as part of a curricular topic.

Children's own writing You can offer these books as strong models for children's own information writing. They can record their observations and findings about a topic, make field notes and sketches, and add extra snippets of information for the reader.

Above all, Read and Wonders are to be enjoyed, and encourage children to develop a lasting curiosity about the world they live in.

Sue Ellis, Centre for Language in Primary Education